entangled bank

entangled bank

a conceptual memoir
of language ecosystems

James Sherry

CHAX
2016

ISBN 978-0-9862640-8-5

Thank you to Casey Mohammad (*Westwind*), Laynie Browne (*Evening Will Come*), Chad Lowther (*Barzakh*), Holly Melgard and Joey Yearous-Algozin (*P-Queue*), Manuel Brito *(Zasterle)*.

On the cover: Detail, *From the Anthropocene #1*, by Judith Belzer, courtesy of the artist and George Lawson Gallery.

On the author biography page:
Author photo by Ben Sherry.

Chax Press is supported in part by the School of Arts & Sciences at the University of Houston-Victoria. We are located in the UHV Center for the Arts in downtown Victoria, Texas.

Chax acknowledges the support of graduate and undergraduate student interns and assistants who contribute to the books we publish. In Fall 2016 our interns are Julieta Woleslagle, Sophia Kameitjo, Errin Maye, and Gabrielle Delao.

This book is also supported by private donors. We are thankful to all of our contributors and members. Please see http://chax.org for more information.

Chax Press
PO Box 162
Victoria, TX 77902-0162
USA

Contents

Genetic Materials

It is interesting to contemplate an entangled bank, clothed with many plants of many kinds, with birds singing on the bushes, with various insects flitting about, and with worms crawling through the damp earth, and to reflect that these elaborately constructed forms, so different from each other, and dependent on each other in so complex a manner, have all been produced by laws acting around us. These laws, taken in the largest sense, being Growth with Reproduction; inheritance which is almost implied by reproduction; Variability from the indirect and direct action of the external conditions of life, and from use and disuse; a Ratio of Increase so high as to lead to a Struggle for Life, and as a consequence to Natural Selection, entailing Divergence of Character and the Extinction of less-improved forms.

> — *Charles Darwin*
> *final paragraph of* Origin of Species, *1859*

Beautiful Poems for My Friends

from poetry readings:

For John Ashbery at 80:
Your poems are so beautiful
Like stars in the night sky
That have become so good
At burning brightly

For Mei-mei Berssenbrugge:
You are beautiful
Well-dressed and beautiful
And read your beautiful poems
Beautifully in a beautiful voice

For Stacy Szymaszek:
You are beautiful
Beautiful and tough
A rebus of beauty
Frankly replying with both parts

For Evelyn Reilly:
You are beautiful
And accurate but chary
Of beauty really
Contradictory though it is

For Bob Holman:
You are beautiful
Fugitive and beautiful
Your motion blurs the edges
Where did you go?

For Norman Fischer:
You are beautiful
Defeated by beauty
Butter on your head
Words in the bellies of moths

For Michael Gottlieb:
You are a beautifully dressed poet
In beautiful, carefully-matched colors
Like a beautiful, green sea turtle
Paddling through beautiful sharp coral

For Ann Lauterbach:
You are so beautiful
When thunder cracks
And you jump beautifully
Coloring the page edge

Lyric Poems

After Hai An but without

The Beautiful
The beautiful, the tongue
The buried, the the,
When some is sum.

The Flows
Earth Day rivers hold over
Modern mourning. Oh thyme
Without hams or whatever,
Wherever they live, scattered,
Stretched to go beyond
From and to
The tributaries.

The Presence
There far to and from,
My so too it rains.
And when the and a appeared,
I realized I had a choice.

Unfinished Symphony
Between living's surmounted palm
Begins an all prevail.
Withdraw cups void between palms,
There should be a fourth line here.

Taking Human Form
I a I as humid I
Nor I near it
But there reviv-ed
How form functions to

Bodily Surprise
Inured to a polar ruler
Nor your confronting
Nor your leaving
But loud material shears.

The Second (Late) Presence
In this one a two and the also,
My they too accept.
Finally, the and this the arrived.
I realize that after again
Continuing to be surprised.

In A Fix
But reach no lettuce
Be friends or move peas flesh
After a encloses the
As it does. It does again!
Once facing us and one away,
Once oneself while we try no stand
And thereafter one other
Until the theory of none bars it.

The Other Was Not Me

Push the I chain without walking.
Touching palms indifferently,
We charter loading,
Waiting, as we push for what?
A tree with a plastic bag?

Standing Hands

Summer without curtains.
In it are the misty folds
Of interference.
I and I there imitating
You being myself:
I my vanish today and
Put my hand through.

Beautiful Poems for My Friends

from Roof's Anniversary Reading

For Nada Gordon:
You are beautiful
And you know it
It's funny too how you
Show it but that's alright

For Erica Kaufman:
You are beautiful
Generous and touch
To help and keep
All you know that's beautiful

For Drew Gardner:
You are beautiful
With surprising detail
In talk and music either
With surface to air missiles

For Kim Rosenfield:
You are beautiful
I caught you looking
Pitiless and forgiving
For thinking you beautiful

For Cecilia Wu:
You are beautiful
To catch a glimpse
But I know you are
Before it could be

For Rob Fitterman:
You are beautiful
Hale and well met
And reworked several times
Without showing any cracks

For Gary Sullivan:
You are beautiful,
Spinning into the ether
Dancing on train roofs
On the string of a kite

For Bruce Andrews:
You are a beauty
A real beaut
Each syllable of beautiful
Has a beautiful, exploitable meaning all its own

For Charles Bernstein:
You are so afraid
To be beautiful except
That shy beauty that glam
Or else beautiful attitude

Passive Voice: Forcing Amaryllis

For the diarist in search of a life
The passive voice tastes good for breakfast.
It somehow lends her work authority.
It rallies nobody's freedom but hope-flack,
That jumping spider, that achy-breaky
Crawl to middle ground
That implies,
As here,
Just how dear she was
To cling to who she was.

An EKG Addressed to Monody's Cloven Hoof
Forced change is climate's government
And with it the pretense of change.
Continuing to think it's only we,
It's only us,
A compromise constructs our towns
And makes the voice ring tone.

While poverty pushes our people passive,
Inequality drives us to the polls,
According to Anna.
It's all we can do unless, unless
We're willing to risk a mess, a mess
As if risk itself assured success
Of our endeavors indeed.

While I'm deciding, women vivify
With figures of endurance and push back,
Ululating where the living operate
Segmented thought
And all the dead know is storytelling.

Citizens motivate through space,
Passively regarding time.
Sweeter far than earthly strain,
Ourselves be bling:
If you refuse to follow the spoor,
It's quite useless to force you.

Shall Pull Us to Glory Like Bricks
These lines voice submerged questions
Like "What?" and "How?" and "Where am I in this?".
Thus the voice of reason cries with winning force,
"wtf?" and "omg". Too often
The power of one organism fails
Even though addressed in mail
And clung to when hearts sail.

Couching nature as bundles and linkages,
Channels and—you can't get more abstract from here—
Leap to march 'neath shriveling swords
To capture intuitions
Such as Bruce has been existing for a long time,
And Deborah is exactly what I would call a role model.

Science, that vast left wing conspiracy
Of avoidance, shifts from *le lot quotidian*
To moral force occurs in parts of a word—am, amar, rill,
An R construed as the whole highlights the limit
Of asserting, repeating, convincing no matter how loud,
Loud with all the facts
Our schooled and slangy children object
That the politics of resistance became a school for shoppers,
Mugwumps awash in righteousness,
Oligarchy disguised as an entangled bank.

To Act With (Apparent) Centrifugal Force
Sparkling centrifuge, Persian miniatures
(meek. o'pasiv.o, voice calling
In the tangled debt (shared/shard
As spinning out rage,
As re-domesticating women after the revolution
Might be a task to resist)) spin.

My meter rounds off numbers,
For what can force or guile,
Their march loose from the rapid cars,
Do to save our world from us?

Long before *The Origin of Species* appeared
Evolution had been reconciling
Entangled thought with banks.
A person : an organism = an idea : a discipline = a poem :
        an ecosystem.
Gone from a passive pursuit

To no longer a voice in the wilderness,
Agency and audience together in devolution.

Font Dog Handbrake Virus!
This poem is dedicated to she
Whose spelling transformed measure.
Whether as vigorous force or sees words,
Cells make markets. *Little Indians*
Grabs the syllable to play.

Country tears in lyric bullets
Fall for my valentine's ringtones
While delusions of reference stream in retribution
For Blake, Milton, Shakespeare:
Bard, polemics, printer's ink.
Welcome to the Subscription Center and enhancement plan:
Tamales of Sparta rolled global.

Faceless Female Persona as Their "Other"
Everywhere you look these days
Funny pregnancy-cake wrestling decorations
Are disappointing women worldwide
While men insist big orgasm
Techniques're bustin' out
Cheat codes on Xbox realty.
Are all these risky idioms networked
Into a single massive missive addressed to you?
Does novel poetry cheat happy sport street
Of a good time had by ill?
How can I talk about someone else,

Except to accept others think otherwise?
Giving-no-quarter ignores
We're all in this together.
Art, as if to saddle a horse
With personal taste, be hers.
How do you account for neighbors?
Civil cases filed against low-protein piety?

Loose Coupling of Theory and Practice
Looking for poetry in all the wrong places,
Loose cannons come with a good time
And extended warranty, so
It's not easy to break those links
To the deeper inner you.

Speak, you poets.
Word up!
Smile at each other.
Negative capability doesn't mean bad attitude.

Loose coupling of theory and practice:
Loosely responsive to spontaneous change,
Coupling through linkages like syntax,
Being is my connector.

What Did Lewis Carroll Do in Mathematics? Or John the Baptist Training Teaches You Not to Lose Your Head

1.
When interfering with power; don't glower.
Let your smile be your umbrella.

Undo their logic a capella.

"Three points are taken at random on an infinite plane. Find the chance of their being the vertices of an obtuse-angled triangle."

Alice Liddell's frame of probability, beyond what's plain,

Is the main chance when we're stuck

Listening to our gut where bacteria speak for us.

2.

What happens to your body when you release control

Of yourself, of your relations, of your views

To write words on purpose,

Not pinning pining hope to the page?

The angel on bended knee humanizes assembly.

Our prophetic mariner walking shoe

Exploits ethical validity

With the method trees use to estimate

And because your first step is often a long one.

3.

"If six cats can kill six rats in six minutes,

How many cats does it take to kill 100 rats in 50 minutes?"

Multiple solutions rule in Kevin Killian's coloring book.

Just how much thought is required to write a poem for art?

You think arbitrary is a problem? Arbitrary is a solution!

Look around you! We've recoupled.

Command-Operated Sheep Cruise aka Cardamom Spoofing

Large blooming amaryllis will have been forced.
The nature of humanity would have been mapped
By the Knicks Albanian hair removal faction, if not
By the Hindu clown penis, safe and alert for donors.
The kingdom of god suffers sore knees,
Tightly coupled. Then we're all set for a ride,
On a night train, teaching liar mechanics to undergrads.
Grievous Dream of Jeannie anti-glare windscreen coating,
And so I learn to write like Alan Davies?

Amaryllis nutrition.
How to accept multiple solutions?
Same not yours to government health care
To diarrhea tractors
To feeding 9 billion amaryllis
Guantanamo amaryllis

Cheap, free, dual-channel, diesel-driven, nutrition-labeled,
hackneyed, anti-theft, Ciceronian, amplified, framed, double,
mobile, absolute, inevitable, ideal, long-stemmed amaryllis!

Beautiful Poems for My Friends

For Richard Tuttle:
You are beautiful
Examining that crack
In the sidewalk carefully
For its delicate spill

For Anne Waldman:
Your arms are beautiful
When you wave them
Over your beautiful head
Recalling us to mind.

For Dan the Painter, not the Brother:
You are beautiful
Saving the world
With theories from the engraved
Desk of the Chin

For Dave and Cody, the Sound Guys:
You are beautiful
Invisible and beautiful
Shining the light in my face.
Please send us those tracks

For Me:
You are beautiful
Dutiful beautiful and
You write beautiful poetry
That everybody says, beautiful.

Mote Removal: Clean Speak

Tidy the noise.
Unclog the glottis.
She speaks louder
Than an extra blanket.

What are we writing for
If not gelato?
It's over there
With the broom she used
To sweep the jelly up.

I cannot believe I've been engaged
In such extraordinary logic.
What then is the ensuing tragedy
When evidence for naturalism sustains
But a bust of Progress on Pegasus
Or sad boys hanging out in redwoods?

Silence passes between us.
I cannot; will not; no no no!
Resistance is futile, fungible
And trains us to consume.

You make me feel like a natural
Appendix at the back of the memorandum
To museum employees
Against levity in the office,
Inspiring aphorism and animated hadiths,
Lived and livid examples of hominid creativity.

There are people willing to speak out for those Americans
Who suffer from the effects of Good Riddance Day
And the Civic Health Index.
It's a perfect standard,
But what are the facts?
They don't stop the reflux of sorrow.
And my signature, trenchant with suppose,
Conveys millions of Turks to clean their buckets
Into the cannibalistic debacle of Syria.
Where must we collapse to change?
Can we think of ourselves differently?

Intensely special in the singular,
Drama creeps into his whimper
Of compliance. How far,
She asked, can I get from myself
Before I am we.
I think of the endless
Survivor luncheons fondly.

To support the interests of those who cannot speak
For themselves, the future is now.
Organ vendor families like Laden and Emaar
Start as discreet poseur neophytes.

Speaking in intelligible words
Instead of tongues builds a following.
How Baba suffered for a devotee's sake.
"Neither could she speak or call,"
While daring to ululate for her rights,

Li'l ole' me showing proper gratitude on the home front,
A human rights competency.

Singing and joking abruptly all stopped
The air in both directions.

I believe these extreme and gruesome crimes
Against the self, however much they abuse my interest,
Although I cannot utter it in polite company,
Their testament hits me on the head.
They clean up entire streets
With great white tunes for little revolts of the spirit,
Whether you're dealing with
(how you deal with (dealing with (dealt with))) inclusion
Or scouring the litterbox for phrases.
It's our duty to remember and commemorate these events.
She extracted a clean, white, cambric handkerchief
And began to weep. "The gravel
On my driveway is always choked with grass."

Beautiful Poems for My Friends

For Barack Obama:
You are beautiful
But we wait and wait like Richard
For the crack to grow a tree
And you to close the gap

For Timothy Geithner:
You are a beautiful
Unsteady transvestite
But how did you convince
Your boss to save the bond holders

From Thanksgiving Dinner after Sandy @ Holleywood
For Margaret Ross:
You are a beautiful poet even absent
It's so poetic when we speak of you
But there is no one we can point to
Here we may say is your spirit

For Helen Ross:
You are so beautiful when you effortlessly
Prepare the perfectly behaved turkey
So we can all eat beautifully
While you're envisioning your next project

For Katherine Ross:
You are beautiful
Surprising those whose vision
Of you: tall rich and beautiful
May not be yours. That's beautiful

For Donald Ross:
You have a beautiful sense of direction
And never seem confused
About your right from your left
Going more than in that direction.

Census of the Filleted Fishes

We're living off the receipts of a good water year…
— Chris Healy, Nevada Division of Wildlife.

Here's something people
find hard to accept: fewer
fish flap in our future.

Among the largest dollar volume of truck shipments were noseless
furniture and agricultural fish products:
policy fact fish, freshwater fact fish, fun fact fish, fun jelly fact fish, fun
star fact fish, gold fact fish gold, interesting fact fish, hawaiian ulua
fact fish, horse sea fact fish fact fish …

Increase the culinary tropical fish life expectancy
With census data, good or bad.
Turkey Thermometer Garden Printing Finalists under Fire!

you`ll need the b-moonfish/b to feed a weird b-chicken sitter,
you`ll see flying fish in towns and dungeons,
those are b-moonfish/b,
when a b-moonfish/b is near you`ll b-b Barbara
Attending a Mozart talk in Pittsfield

Used Electrical Breakers
Census just a dip in the ocean: Scientists are taking a census of
marine life that has revealed thousands of previously undiscovered
species, and how pollution and global warming affect life
underwater

A total of 3750 tigers.
3304 Baby Clown Fish
Apartment Car

Show Television Invitation Shower Wedding Wording Grandee
        Lava Lamp Calculators
latter day saint ancestry church mormon ancestry clown fish
        ancestry
drainage creel homage lucky end

Chip n Fish H Salt Fish Caner
Looks like Fish Caner that I am
hoping the same Fish Caner
who in 1881 was a basket maker ...

Fish Taco
A nose count can confect Bolshevik zumba working she-males
@ a sundown luau for Maui nitrates in fish ...

Where to Fish When the Leaves Are Interracial?
Advertisers Run Away from Dogs.

The Maria Lopez fish can live for months out of water

The Scubapoppy
How Many Fish in the Sea?
Census of Marine Life Shows Jellies Replacing Fish
Hang'em by their knack for self-trumpeting
They batter my heart with demand
And we will know much better what we do not know
Identifying the
determined fish, each "worth" about $3000.00

Wrinkle creams: Your guide to younger looking poetry
Iron them, burnish them, don't let them flap around too much
Perhaps there might be one good one in the bunch

More than three times as many blacks live in prison cells than
        in college dorms,
Platform shoe gold fish concusses denizens

Phone Psychics Comparison)
Educators who would like to use this activity should email
Bill.Crowley@esc9.net for the fish ID form and census form.
Please place the words "Fish ID" in the subject line. Author:
scubapoppy Keywords: marine life science ...

YouTube :: Tag // marines - http://youtube.com/rss/
        tag/+marines.rss

White Fish 10 Dec 2007 by Alexa
The population was 5032 at the 2000 census. It is home to
a ski resort called Whitefish Mountain Resort. Whitefish.com
Your Guide to Adventure (800) 985-3765. Whitefish Montana
Lodging at The Lodge at Whitefish Lake Year round lodging.
...

fish net - http://fish-net.betta-fish-ebooks.info

Advance know-how where to fish7 Dec 2007 by Victoria
How Many Fish in the Sea? Census of Marine Life Launches
First Report. Are jellies replacing fish? And we will know much
better what we do not know - identifying the ... We invite
additional worldwide support and participation to advance ...

christian fish - http://christian-fish.betta-fish-ebooks.info

Fact: According to the 2010 US census, there are over 221
million adults in our country. Over 100 million of them (roughly
46% of the population) are single. Consideration: Perhaps
there might be one good one in the bunch? ...

Hazel's Girl Power Blog - http://www.girlpowerblog.com/hazel

All Jelly Blackout
Eating all the anchovies
Clogging the nuclear power plant water intakes
It's jellies all the way down!

Beautiful Poems for My Friends

For My Boss Frank:
You are beautiful when
My paycheck is pregnant with beautiful bonuses
And of course work is much more beautiful
When I'm beautiful and rich

For My Landlord Tenny:
You are beautiful when my rent
Is low and the light outside stays on
So I can see my key going in
The lock cold and beautiful

For Toyota Motors:
You are beautiful when my car runs beautifully
And doesn't use beautiful gas to pay for
The Saudis to plan their beautiful
Attacks and poison our beautiful planet.

For Deborah Thomas:
You are so beautiful
That I'd better be careful of
Your beauty because I'm
At risk of your being beautiful

For Ben Sherry:
Beauty is in the eye
Of the bee-holder and the first person
Shooter is beautiful
After you do your homework

Formal Invention Predicts
the Invasion of Art by Content

The banks heard enough shoes
Drop for a centipede.
The regulators reclined.
And every unplugged person moved in on credit.
Meanwhile, Alchemical Republicans seem
Gratified that the toothsome negotiate among them.
Hype want, stim want, make'em want want
And you control the future. LOL.

Formal rulings replaced by psychological tools for obliging us to do what the system requires. As Hayek said, "that which is the result of human action but not of human design…" Good old Hayek, clapping one invisible hand.
A spontaneous order:

Gravity Holds a Shield for You
Your Shih Tzu's hair appointment
With Ma and dot rental birds,
Then python rpm gratuity,
Unmatched braces bracing
For invasion subtleties,
Sips cocktails for ingrates.

What Is the Best Way to Get Rid of Hickeys?
Sea slug, bubble cliché, gasoline computer and
Amorous exercises exorcize rebar whipped ferns.

When the mothership lands
Its old shape invites the biosphere to try it on

With the potential to slow climate change
By eliminating the need to burn wood, coal and oil,
Thereby avoiding invasion of the objectifying logic of markets.

Posh Spill Sorrow

Vast joins ensue
With tectonic scorch,
A long speech by his citizens
About how important he is to them.
I nominate the buttress,
A nearly limitless planet even under environmental strictures
And no guilt trip to speak of
From a peppery hostage with the spy chip under her skin:
The goddess Athena buys all shares currently in the hands
Of private investors in a patent survey of hospital rock.
Its shoe to shoe and toe to too as tuxedos teetotal,
As the assets of Bell's palsy avalanche
Down your face of sex position maps
Showing rivers and mountains without
The elephant's trunk filled with sweet regrets.

"This website will help you find out everything you need to know...."

Neutral milk hostel!
Paris Hilton expects more mitochondria in muscle cells,
Google inflatable spätzle in Calgary,
Rubber hospital accommodation laws
Of dependence, of assimilation,
Of poems like Racine's "tired of being loved
He wants to be feared"
While soap operas free Russian brides.

White House Sushi Policy

Joy invades what we thought would be
An oligarchic cut up cake.

A unitard-only unabomber golf course prepares the way for a
revolt against how she feels about being touched, that form
of society through prom sex, a melancholy, stifling night for an
invasion of recycled references used by middle aged poetics
manufacturers.

Climate change scenarists smelled my boat coming along the
protozoan condos on the eve of Babar's invasion of Delhi but
were afraid to say the obvious.

Then the bridegroom voided on his jet ski.

The multicultural optimist flaunted my wondrous, ponderous
pearl bladed leader shredder,

Bringing down the wrath of people seeking fairness and
opportunity to steal from their neighbors.

Cape Fear Falafel

Libri per bambini:
Our *Morte D'Arthur* sentiment simulator
Ignores internal contractions and
Who distributes accumulated surplus.
But mawkishness aside, we love our friends in spite.
Workshop the revolution!

Real estate renters in non-reproducing communities
Beg for a fiery ending.
One level of our mind is constantly active, yes sir.
Invaluable, variable, invasion, invertebrate:
Better loathe our Swamp Thing Festival
Than think badly of me for

Vanity, vanity, your matter is metaphor.

For metaphor is a physical thing in bodies

An inference skill,

Like your Mesopotamian calendar

And standards for the ecosystem bridge

Where no birds sing.

So that while ecosystem is a metaphor

It remains a measure, not an aura,

When a thought too much for logic inspires.

The ancient Chinese abacus uses

Parataxis where parallel prevails

And hypotaxis when changing levels in the hierarchy rather than making a joke about connections.

But fear of being wrong, of the steel crèche,

Of it simply being inherent, i.e., natural phenomena

And not how special we are,

Gives us pause, standing

Before the Chamber of Medusas,

Our deadbeat whole art sandwiches.

We love poetry but does it love us?

Figure out an Ending

When the Hebrew Prophet predicts that "all the nations and peoples of the earth shall serve him" or "the people of the Saints of the Most High," must we understand that he means thereby the nations of Arizona, North Korea, institutional controls on conscience and oligarchy exposed
     by Citizen's United?

Or does he mean ethical leadership?

And what are the perils of that?

Globalization and the Role of You

Stick to gene mod surgery,
A series of cunning binaries,
When given the choice of you or the planet
Remember the choice is posed by a group
With interests in ingredients
Not an individual, not the world,
When balancing conditions threaten
To be a continuous poem
And not end conveniently in periods:
Wake up; it's about you.

III. Conceptual Flarf[1]

"Tagmosis / Prosody (extending parataxis)"

The Volta: Poetics Archive, Resources, & Pedagogy
www.thevolta.org/thevolta-resources.html

"**Tagmosis / Prosody (extending parataxis**)." The
Consequence of Innovation: 21st Century Poetics. Edited by
Craig Dworkin. New York: Roof Books, 2008

III. a. Tagmosis/ Prosody Extending

GZIP]
1078 shak 929 encephalopathic 925
antidisestablishmentarianism 922 ...

File Format: Unrecognized
... proxemics 20 **prosodic** 20 proponents 20 pronoid 20 promises
20 preverbial **......** 3 tahsils 3 tahina 3 tahi 3 tagolog 3 tago 3
tagmosis 3 tafy 3 tafurn 3 **...**
www.dict.org/380knotfound.txt.gz - Similar pages - Note this

III. b. Tagmosis / Prosody

GZIP]
1078 shak 929 encephalopathic 925
antidisestablishmentarianism 922 ...

File Format: Unrecognized
... proxemics 20 **prosodic** 20 proponents 20 pronoid 20 promises
20 preverbial **......** 3 tahsils 3 tahina 3 tahi 3 tagolog 3 tago 3
tagmosis 3 tafy 3 tafurn 3 **...**
www.dict.org/380knotfound.txt.gz - Similar pages - Note this

III. c. Tagmosis Parataxis

Cómo instruye comparar conceptos
- [Translate this page]
Sintaxis, **parataxis**, **tagmosis** y sintagma. El diccionario de la
Real Academia sólo ofrece dos definiciones del término sintaxis:
"Parte de la gramática que **...**
www.correodelmaestro.com/anteriores/2002/abril/sentidos71.
htm - 14k - Cached - Similar pages - Note this

[RTF]
A a-, an-: without abyss, alogical, anarchy ETC. abax: reckoning ...

File Format: Rich Text Format
A. a-, an-: without. abyss, alogical, anarchy ETC. abax: reckoning
board. abacist, abacus. agaqoV: good. Agatha, agathism,
kalokagathia **...**

faculty.muhs.edu/greenwald/FinalGreekDict.rtf - Similar pages -
Note this

III. d. Prosody Extending Parataxis

As Wesling puts it, the major failure of poetics, the one that
subsumes all others, has been its lack of "hermeneutical first
principles" (1996: 37) in http://www2.bc.edu/~richarad/lcb/wip/
rc1.html

[1] The piece uses the method of flarf to select a vocabulary through
an internet search on increasingly limited strings, starting with
"Tagmosis / Prosody (extending parataxis)," but also then the method
of conceptualism by appropriating exactly what the string produced
onto the pages above. The search was performed in October 2009 and
results have changed.

Parallel Anthem

first	invest	submerge	cry
you	wisely	souls	out-loud
wave	in	in	in
the	the	the	The
american	future	negative	expected
flag	you	existence	bottom
until	end	with	nowhere
you	up	space	in
feel	losing	between	sight
nothing	your	myself	dream
but	shirt	and	of
opportunity	anyway	paradise	tumble

and	oh-oh	mine	Suckers
the	say	eyes	Deviate
rockets	can	have	Adulterated
red	you	seen	Tinct
glare	see	the	Shocks
the	by	glory	The
bombs	of	the	Ground
bursting	dawn's	heaving	Redolence
in	early	coming	Up
air	light	of	Pride

link	force	seduce	And
cash	leadership	changes	Retort
infusions	also	to	Process
to	cormorant	to	come
performance	sufferer	to	support
as	some	the	the
solution	pain	coordination	people

Polonialism: An Anonymous Paragraph

Circa 1963

In Promulgating your Esoteric Cogitations, or Articulating Superficial Sentimentalities, and philosophical and psychological observations, beware of Platitudinous Ponderosity. Let your conversation possess a Clarified Concision, Compacted Comprehensibleness, Coalescent consistency, and a Concatenated Cogency. Eschew all Conglomerations of Flatulent Garrulity, Jejune Babblement and Asinine affectations. Let your extemporaneous Discantings and unpremeditated Expiations have intelligibility, without Rhodomontade or Thrasonical Bombast. Sedulously avoid all poly-syllabical Profundity, a Pompous Prolixity and Ventriloqual Verpidity. Shun *double entendre* and Prurient Jocosity, whether obscure or apparent.

Nature Red in Parallel or The Politics of Fear

This was more of the terrible unknown.
— Jack London

we	they	He	you
toil	overturn	Surge	singe
in	through	Into	about
vast	mirthless	lifeless	savage
silence	desolation	Smile	frozen
of	like	Into	over
the	A	Some	one
sphinx	memory	Abyss	W

Out	of	erroneous	frantic
The	one	This	scrutinizing
fryingpan	fool	foredoomed	blasphemy
and	also	But	then
into	overall	Terror	in
passion	suspicion	Gloom	future

pause	urge	Stumble	collapse
at	of	At	toward
the	an	His	her
mouth	impulse	simultaneous	consecutive
of	To	About	around
cave	nuclear	disagreement	theocracy

we	nationalized	women	completely
conserve	Banks	exploit	cynical
but	recover	Here	bond-holders
suppressed	link	benefit	Islam
slowly	innocent	america's	villagers
intention	rage	Finally	anymore
of	decide	citizens	rend
incent	rises	Fate	Pol-Pot-ash-(ish)

Coda:

make	walls	passage	recede
the	translucent	and	flickering
lights	light	approach	outside
sprawl	fear	alarm	wall
through	growth	evolution	leaped
yielding	backward	solid	change

Spelling Suggestions for Brandon Brown's Obscurer Words in Flowering Mall

Proxy Lives of the Poets

Enfin, pour compléter ton rôle de Marie,
Et pour mêler l'amour avec la barbarie,

We were unbridled
Before *overtakeless*
Form took a while to
Break into song.
Are our actual vibrancies theirs
Or can "The Ideal and the Actual Life" share?

Vampires in Frisco

une outre aux flancs gluants, toute pleine de pus!

Escaping strife with Smiley Face,
Famished for pop music's taste,
Intent at first a bit *opaque-ish*,
Lurking in the Mission victorious,
"To die, to be really dead,
That must be glorious!"

Dusky Dukes at Daybreak

Ô vers! noirs compagnons sans oreille et sans yeux,

Not much to hear or see under there, abandoned
Light "crawling through the damp earth".
Glance at social media *hateration*,
Like marmalade, the furor in the bureau of cure-alls.

All ears and eyes yearn for a curvy verse line,
Call it shade or everyday cloud.

The Howl of Representatives
Tu n'es pas digne qu'on t'enlève
À ton esclavage maudit

Enough proxy, gimmie moxie!
Signify real people's real lives
When you embody *hypostasy*.
Sadly, representation will not expire
As poetry and biology desire.

Porno Poetics
A l'air d'un moribond caressant son tombeau

I foresee hardening subject to davening.
Surrenders tricky tributes,
A uteric utterer, the horror, the honor
Of having been harbored
In boyish humility,
While kayoed at the cash kiosk,
Where *topplings* show security's
False futurity. Momentary, eternal:
Up the body politic!

Flaneur Foodie
Les baumes pénétrants que ta panse féconde
Garde au coeur altéré du poète pieux;

Omigod amigos!
Stuff my face with freebee frijoles.

And let us lettuce it, too!
I wuz led awry by ample fries,
Rassle-ing snails and cockles
In a cloudburst in a cabbage patch
In retinas retinue of potluck pot lickers.
Puntarelle buoys anchovy
In a sauce from Jon Bon Jovi.
Whereupon a soupcon of live codlings
Evokes twinkie nostalgia from offal-eating yokels.
This sugary sweet from our memorable Octavian,
His bees beget flexures and answers Bayesian.

Correct Politics

[notre] supplice
Aura-t-il jamais une fin?

Who wants the earth
Once they let
The meek inherit
What's left of it?

Does the pitter pat of protester-
Protectors pester you?
Let me mace your grace about the face.
Could the state be more *woesome*?
Get thee to the museum, go!

Bird Watching in the Oakland

Ces robes folles sont l'emblème
De ton esprit bariolé;
Folle dont je suis affolé,

Oil it, owlet, disembowel it

Unless you frown on motley.

Or do you want Towhee tacos?

As scholars sipped *swallowship*,

Trust a lark to park dark in your throat

"To new and unthought pleasures."

The Rein Scribe Notes the Bloke's Jokes

La Circé tyrannique aux dangereux parfums

About signature binding

Boy Circe's circlet curls

With promises to novices;

Young *crackerlet* tenders.

His autopoiesis *reinscribes* titles.

It tantalizes tonal eyes with frozen fries,

Recycling cries about the biosphere.

The human as a system and as a person

Of trees and dollars freed by technologies.

There oughta be a law.

Occupy the Recovery

…dans ton antre
Tremble de froid

Once homeowners had known loans,

Originary and proper paper.

Now banks own your signature,

Subsumption juridical,
Financed from mine to swine.
Note: elites will never resign.
The rascals rustle
Whatever we let 'em.
Their little lives are fun to them
They don't look back,
While most require a little hearth fire
And an occasional fish dish
Would be nice, too, perhaps
And a bottle of coddle
To cuddle, Harold.
A consular tonsure would be fine sir,
As the *dandiacal* poet would have it,
A creature, or what you'd call an office.

Just Bein' Him in Bedlam
Dans le bric-à-brac jusqu'au cou,

Sharper that
Than the cash track
Of a pop attack
On social cemetery soil.
Up to the neck in tchotchkes,
While death watches of *precarity*
"Lurch back and forth across the span,"
Yearning for learning and hearkening
To veneers and sneers about the same fears
Of belief that keeps persons on tenterhooks,
Puling while we opt for *vampiric* release
From dissolving superlatives.

Tunis

Si, le corset brutal emprisonnant tes flancs

Patiently, patently, potently,
Picnolepsy helps us see trucks,
Entangling what you'd want
With the "paparazzial" burning
In a struggle to be free
Of abyssal blips on the news.
Who owns your daddy?

Disforested in the Moorish morass,
Wrenching henchmen from their penchant
For replacing one tyranny with another,
We plant Libya in lingerie.
Your biscuit artist retains rattan.
Kelp oleo with chairs
Slays all *auratic* ages and salvages
Last week, wreaked in Tintin.
Him a Muslim in muslin even.

Weapons of Mass Distraction

De ces vindicatifs et monstrueux reptiles

Something's wrong with the official version of events,
"Participat[ing] in the disastrous delirium of finance,"
Whose austere teeth renew a mother misconstrual:
That there is one, when actual is many,
Medea in media, your personal reverse ATM.

How do they get you to see what they want you to see?
Why "trust corporate media"? Of course!
Of course, what they say is true to them,
Tho leakage and spills control
Tips on intricacies so redacted
No doubt by *rearers* of events. I wonder
How public value burns to be!

Trains Articulation

(Please impute your own subject matter to this poem
remembering what you don't know about it.)

It's conceivable
And appropriately seasonable,
Even if results
Aren't all that reasonable?

What's the weather
Between my fingers?
I dunno, ague?
Arguing, I'm sure; with Mondays.
Yeah, I knew, censure:
I don't remember anything about it.
They made me do it.
I was drunk.
Just following orders.

Suddenly it's quite quiet on the train
Except, of course, for breathing and tracks.
But the story gets longer.
I don't know whether clearer
But I'm saying you might want to hear her out.

Line me up with a corner.
Box me into come again.
I'm not and then feign,
Even if you claim

You are. Yet, I persist,
But don't want to wait.

A departure of the whole cell,
Actually going against it,
Tonight. Not a planet at all
Going out with the light.

Darwin's Dog Reels

for Calvin Trillin

Memo on "Divergence of Character"

From: Occupy

To: Jamie Dimon, Ginni Rometty, Jeffrey Immelt, Michael Duke, Rex Tillerson, Fu Chengyu, Jiang Jiemin, Akio Toyoda, Henri de Castries, Michael Williams, Ivan Glasenberg, Warren Buffet, Daniel Akerson, Brian Moynihan, Geesung Choi, et. al.:

You shall not want
Faith to form
from firm's indifference

for when business fails
to provide for persons
the cons surface.

As nation states fade under corporate
Pressures, people fill the gap
and the rough engulfs you, too.

Too much success breeds contempt,
the other side of moral hazard.
RSVP…

"Struggle for Life"

Vegan Dog Reel

We rip plants from their soil
Tearing out their roots with speed
Yet the plants are not deceased
When we chop them into pieces
And burn them in hot grease
Then crush them to pulp
And flush them down our greedy
Hot acid with a gulp.

Spiritual Markets
My faith is my insurance
And this I do propose:
World markets do assure us.
Jesus, monetize my soul!

Occupational Hazards
Voter ids cost 25k;
S'alright, long as I get paid
And you love my poetry;
Of course, those prereqs!
The solution is transparent banks.
If you build one, you get no thanks.
Instead folks wanna own ideas,
Barkers, snake charmers, Shia careerists,
Guys in hats that hold the bats.

Everybody agrees on the Way
Until they start to do it. That's ok,
But then ideals depart
And the pissing contests start
With character smears:
What realpolitik means,
Must be in their genes
An assertion fought by queens
And trans in their glad rags.
Leaders' principles flag
Who pursue class robbery.
Folks are left with only poverty,
Oh, and poetry. That's different.

I Choose You, Pikachu: a commencement address

I love writing about nothing
It's the only thing I know anything about

A "Ratio of Increase so high as to lead
to a Struggle for Life,"
with leaders squiring this view
Toward new highs conceived in labor
And dedicated to the preposition
Of
That which we are.

Turned pages to a great bafflement of that flow
Where choice is politics
And certain literature ironically limits it,
Testing whether class control or one's character
So conceived by advertisement
Can prevail against the sanctity of which human life.

And behind this charming little idea
I find a charming big idea:
Choice like self
Can be artfully molded
Beyond the polar bores
To shed the past imperfect
And craft ideals of our right to choose,
As if singular replaced plural.

Information, that moral commodity
That shapes now,
And we are told of where and when the how
And many vogue,
Imposed by our species state.

To say momentous vagaries are measured,
And not by us, conflicts with choice
Of weapons and on the largest scale we don't,
Though we try.

The small scale collective change
That government invokes, the choice,

No longer conditions our future on past mistakes
And sometimes comes after the carpe diem.

But now we come to our own life
And what shall I say of that?
What drives us to a vigorous frame
Where deception runs vainly for the shadows?
What action saves us from ourselves
Knowing when to choose and when to yield
And when to swig or we shall
Perish from the earth?

Hedge Fund Hooker Wins Hotdog Eat-a-thon or "Variability from the Indirect and Direct Action"

The Tea Party

Excellent, excellent!
Oh, absolutely,
Totally abandoned.
Good job!

Occupy, Bank

Occupy bank models
Social interactions reducing
The cost of profit.

I buy a chicken.
The bank helps

Without inviting fear and greed
To dinner.
I rent an apartment.
The bank helps
With character loans
And teaches me how to work
With my landlord.
My business expands.
The peer to peer network
Finds a creditor
On the internet
To take a risk
Based on my language.
But sadly Occupy vacated.
Fixed on only one bond
Among many humanities,
It collapsed from purity
Which never succeeds as praxis
And failure to understand
That anarchy includes mutual aid
As well as independent action.

Chameleon

When I hear coughing
I become a doctor
When I see violence
I become a cop
When I smell fish
I become a chef
When I want to be rich and famous
I write a poem
When I touch you
I become myself

"Growth with Reproduction"

The fly that flies all
The time doesn't die

Cybersecurity

What ho!
I spring to sleight of hand and lock
Our ip addresses from outside shock.
This layer of meaning disguises
Continued traffic and realizes
Our link by restraining those
Compromises we'd have to compose
If we were joined by voice
As by choice.

So-o-o-o,
Cache all your bandwidth
And bind to my verse
A course toward obsession
And something much worse.

Um,
Beyond urgent need to do,
How do
I know what you
Could tell who
Can find a mode to
Drop me on my route.

The Gravity of Politics

If Rick Perry wins his erection
I am only three letters away
From his oval orifice.
If Donald Trump wins this hand
The anger against leaders
Who have taken too much
And given too little in return surges.
The message is the message,
Its envelope rife with addresses
And the body pulling your chain.

What persists leads away from the source:
The gravity of politics.

Darwin

Why
Aren't
We
Nicer
To
Each
Other
On
This
Bullet
Train
To
The
Grave

"Extinction of Less-improved Forms"
Leaving no layers between
Content and Transport.
Where are you going
With that bag of money?

Obliterate: sustaining replaces excellence
Social life: absconded
Stolen interludes lose
to your cyclopean gaze.

The question now is how
to mend tutelage by changing tutors
when the lesson is recited
Face time lost to face book.
Is it different than Gutenberg?

Survivors of the last extinction
were unexpected ubiquities.
Will this time save fortresses
more than distributed networks?

"Ratio of Increase"
For sake of love, I washed my hands
of it, in decades' maudlin excursions,
Hastening on stranger trains
to soothe a rough measure.

My child sits on King Cole's table,
while he complains of service breaches,
Ogled by Alice and a boiled egg,
Rehashing all Vegata's rages
and Stanley Kowalski's simple renege,
running with bulls through Beethoven's lea
across Long John's treasured sea.

Time bound lives lean on Chippendale railings.
Shards of elm on the grave, gravel immanence
Seep in fading notes, rests too brief to pause
Complete a spontaneous pulse.
Clothed with many species of shrubberies
with finches singing on the yews,
with lady clocks and dragon flies flitting about,
with c. elegans crawling through the damp earth
to reflect these elaborately constructed forms.

The Ball

The ball was hit by the ballplayer
Who no longer cared for the game
His thought process was far away
On a preposition at the end of the sentence

On its surface I don't know
Where it starts
As it approaches
I don't know where it ends

Suddenly death is everywhere

Suddenly death is everywhere
Well maybe not suddenly
It's been years
Maybe always,
No, there was a while
When I didn't think about it!

The police call, the medical examiner calls
The father calls, the step-mother calls
The painter calls, the sculptor calls
The lawyer calls, the accountant calls
The dentist is called, the doctor is called
The funeral home is called
A message thirty years old
Still means frustration

Progeny topsoil
Telephonic justification
Considering all the wars, diseases, toxins
Still not enough humans die to make a dent
Except in themselves
Just going along as if
There wasn't an end
That does not diminish the relationship
Between humans and our surroundings.

Death arises from the same forces
As those that allow us to exist
For a time ecstatically breathing.
Death confirms it.

In Memoriam

You will not care because you will not exist.
— Lucretius

No more memorial services for me
Where poets intone their own poems
Pretending to revere the dearly departed.

So here's the story:
My friends age, sicken and expire; what else to do?
Finally, I croak, too.
And none whose commemorative
I graced with my presence
Graces it with their presence.
The one I really care about we'll miss.

Written in a Subway Stalled under the East River

Stacy Doris' death happened too recently for me to compose my views on our literary relationship so I have chosen to describe the events and changing states that we shared. I expose my own mental condition believing that it will illuminate Stacy's status as a poet dying although I do acknowledge the problem of linking my experience to hers.

We're puppets since words

sing through us from wherever not

ours into everyone we're screwed

I'm not sure I can tell the difference between what I did, what I said and what I wrote, so you will forgive me if I fail to distinguish or even merge the separates. They converge anyway in grief. But I will nevertheless try to compose myself by giving you a range of observations about Stacy, about our exchanges, and about me to expose her. Your opinion can cohere around them.

At one point Stacy calls me or writes me that she has had surgery on her fibroids. Upon biopsy, doctors found a rare cancerous form of a common benign tumor. She speaks in an outraged, sardonic voice about their incompetence. But she is optimistic that they can get rid of all cancerous cells with another surgery. We talk for an hour on the phone. She comes to NY and does a reading, seated with her upper body turned toward the audience in a strange venue somewhere in the 20s. It's not the poetry site we're used to, and it feels like an alien planet. Stacy remains as wonderful as Johnny Carson and Bette Midler in a poetry sort of way.

Then I get a diagnosis of prostate cancer. Like Stacy's my prior treatment was questionable; I begin to connect to Stacy as patient. My diagnosis was delayed due to a catch in the process. Initially, the doctor put me on hormones to resolve an ED problem instead of performing a biopsy, only to discover later that the hormones stimulated cancer growth: when he finally did the biopsy all 12 samples are positive. The urologist tells me that I will have surgery, then radiation, then androgen therapy. I am depressed by the news but optimistic that I can beat it. The post-surgical biopsy shows three areas of extra-capsular extension but no lymph node or seminal vesicle involvement, implying only local metastasis. I talk to upbeat prostate cancer survivors who send me verses about disease; life can continue. Charles visits me while I'm recovering, and we assert the primacy of alertness.

Stacy calls to tell me that she is going to Israel to undergo an experimental immune system booster that helps three out of four people. We talk about her nagalase levels and the blood types where GC-Maf can help improve apoptosis. We talk like that a lot. We read sentences from technical papers to each other and laugh about the implications of a poorly turned phrase. We talk about it on several occasions. Mostly we talk to keep each other company because most others are just sympathetic, trying to help, and we like our doomed company.

The overlap of our Venn diagrams increases. I contact the doctor in Israel who says he usually treats advanced cancer, but that his treatment can be more effective with minimal cancer such as mine. Stacy starts her treatments. She tells me about giving herself injections by pinching the skin of her stomach. I am totally grossed out, but "James," she says, "it's nothing." We talk about the doctor in Israel; she is impressed by him and his knowledge. She says he's the real thing. I am convinced.

I go to Israel with Deborah and Ben who visit the West Bank while I visit the doctor. We come back to NY with a bag of drugs. Then I start my treatment, and the needles are oddly reassuring. The pin prick, too, reassures. We are both optimistic. We talk and talk swapping soothing medical jargon. We suppose it means something. Really we're just a bit lonely; no one is committed like a patient. I tell her the joke about the pig and the chicken at breakfast. She doesn't find it humorous.

For a long time after our treatments are finished we do not speak as if speaking would invoke recurrence. We exchange some letters and fall away from each other. The Stacy part of me is cured.

Hey Team! Now you've arrived

at so-called death. Dig in and relish it.

Months pass and someone writes or says that Stacy has recurrence. I call her and we talk and talk. This time we both know what it means, but don't say it. She talks about her doctor in the Bay area that she doesn't like and her doctor in Boston that she likes. Her voice sounds more distant. I am worried for both of us, but I try to distance myself from her, to disengage, because I convince myself that her cancer was advanced and mine remains minimal. I don't want to be dragged down by our community and try to be independent. My PSA remains undetectable <.05ng/ml. I feel safe and threatening at the same time.

I extrapolate from her disease to mine realizing that she is not me, but the link is established. I make a thousand other linkages; my mind turns into an inference machine, maybe was always. The level of the linkage needs to be examined but often goes unexamined. They all feel threateningly the same. More thoughts cross my mind than I can separate. Anacoluthon dominates my sentence structure. You think I am writing about me but I'm writing about her because no one wants to burden you with their death. We're too well bred.

Stacy has a variety of other medical treatments. We talk, more surgery, we talk, and I can tell by her tone of voice that she is beginning to fade. The connections between the treatments and her reasoning become more flimsy, sometimes jump, sometimes the gap is too far. Sometimes she makes a connection to some reference that only she sees. The chemo isn't shrinking the tumor. The tumor is pushing against her liver, her kidney. Reassurance doesn't make a difference to her.

Frankness doesn't work either; it's inappropriate. I say that Chet is a great father; her kids are alright. She says I'm not supposed to say those kinds of things to her. I try to separate my fear for me from my fear for her. I think I succeed in that I focus on many other things. I take on other activities. I occupy myself with Occupy. I start new writing projects. I don't call Stacy. I'd rather feel guilty than magnetized to her.

Unsupported catastrophes

hitting the agility exhausted

so fury only's left offence

On Feb 1, 2012, I get a call or an email from Rob that Stacy has died. I am sad and worried because I had a blood test that same day. Have I truly disconnected? Rob says that when he visited Stacy that they only talked about other things. I don't understand him.

The next day, Groundhog Day, I get my test results. My PSA has risen from <.05 to .05. I see Stacy's shadow. I think about Bill Murray and Stacy. I remember what Drew says about fighting his diabetes more aggressively than the doctors. I make an appointment for three weeks later to retest because, I am assured, there are frequent bulges in PSA readings. It's a bad three weeks. This is no longer about Stacy, but you may hereby know what Stacy felt, because no one wants to burden you with their death; we're too well bred.

I race through all possible reasons, all possible outcomes. I think about radiation. It will burn my bladder and rectum and will not heal for a year. I will have to wear diapers again. My sexual function, slowly improving since surgery, will fail again, this time for good. My recurrence, coming as it does in the second year after surgery, implies remote metastasis and the need for androgen therapy that will cause significant cognitive issues. All I want is to be alert. No, I want to be alert and sexy. No, I want to be alert, sexy and cancer free.

I need to take action on my own behalf and think of Drew again. I talk to Michael frequently since he had prostate cancer before me but no extra capsular extension. I make an appointment with the urologist to discuss the various approaches. He has been prescribing supplements to suppress cancer growth and improve apoptosis: mushroom, turmeric, pomegranate, red wine thank you. This time his reassurances imply that he doesn't see any good alternatives for me; he appears fatalistic who once was adaptive. Then he says his son is dying of cancer. He says he's there for me.

I think about my retirement nest egg; I think about how my family can survive without me; I think about the gloating survivors; I think about the sad survivors; I think about survivors who identify with my situation; I think about survivors who dismiss my situation as not about them. I think about unfinished projects. I think about daily radiation, pain and weakness. I think about my body slowing down with radiation, then rebounding, then slowing again with androgen therapy. Then rebounding and then slowing again with death. My mind jumps from one thought to another; the usual montage clips shorten.

I focus on my body; I move my body slowly and focus. My mind settles down. I resent that I can control my mind but not the cancer. I stop concentrating thinking to find a solution by letting my subconscious do the work. I realize that all my life has been the same situation: connect to someone else to understand what's going on. I think that is like my doctors' reassurances: helpful but implying that there are no alternatives. I think about *Invasion of the Body Snatchers*, *Animorphs*, Yuri Geller. I remember that people say they cure cancer with laughter. I think about how it feels to die, I think about pain, humiliation, suicide. This all takes about three seconds. Then it repeats in a different order with the same conclusion. Then it repeats in a different order with a different conclusion. Then it starts repeating in the same order with the same conclusion. Like Churchill said of Americans I always come to the right conclusion after trying all the others. Then I go do something else.

Every time I stop the thoughts recur, mostly the same ones; I am making no progress; I am annoyed with my limitations. I read voraciously. I focus on alternatives and think about the immune system boosters I have taken. Are there others? All the papers I find are vague and not encouraging. I read about the immune system and realize that innate responses can't find the cancer. There is also adaptive immunity with its macrophages, lymphocytes, killer T-cells, and helper t-cells that can't find the cancer. The cytokines produced by the cancer disguise it from the immune system, an additional function that the immunotherapy has to provide. There are so many components that have to be stimulated and brought to bear on the cancer cells. How can the cytokine disguise be overcome and the cancer be seen as non-self, removing my connection to my body, removing my connection to Stacy? I despair about immunotherapy. I think about Stacy going through these same thought processes. I wonder exactly how she feels about them. Oops! I am wondering how she *felt* about them.

After three weeks of speculation about deterioration and death, I have another blood test. The PSA is now <.05. I am bumping along the bottom. I will live without radiation, without hormone therapy. I spend some money. I reassure the friends like Anne and Evelyn who I told about my rising PSA. I wonder if this rise and fall is a precursor to an increase that is more permanent or if it's just stimulation from my breasts and urethra. I equate this pattern to the 10-year bond prices at the end of a 30-year bull market in bonds. I equate it to stirring ingredients into a recipe; they merge and become one: a mixture, a solution, a suspension. All the other meanings of these words connect to their analog in the disease.

Figures explain lives

that's why cheering counts.

I equate the pattern to Stacy's. I think about how she must have felt and wondered if she was as afraid as I am. Well, of course, that's what it meant that we spoke for hours about the facts and minutes about how we felt about them. Did she acknowledge to herself that she was dying or did her thoughts jump from extreme to extreme to extricate herself from the growing cancer. Each time it was cut out, it regrew. Each time it regrows it becomes more plausible. Editing. How can she not have known? We're going to die anyway, but seeing it coming specifically is hard to do without flinching.

Then I am scheduled for my regular blood test again and again it has risen to .05… This time I am inured, accepting the step closer. It seems much more reasonable that it's just bumping along the bottom, dithering between < and = .05. If I objectify my body as the disease, it is still a thing, or has disease become my person a la Hans Castorp? And if next time it's .06, what will I do? The doctors will still disagree and the choice will be up to me: radiate or not, androgen therapy or not. How can my decision be more informed than the doctor? And yet they want me to make the decision like choosing a tie; therefore, they must think I know more. But how can I know more when my mind is flighty?

I read and read and get diverse opinions: but death is not diverse when it's yours. Imagine how Stacy must have felt gradually sinking into her disease, into her death. Each time death appears closer, becomes a more plausible conclusion even though it's always the conclusion. The doctors keep giving her choices to make, a bizarre bazaar with our bodies the wares. The doctor holds our hands while we die; I had hoped to be paying for a cure, and maybe I will not recur; maybe I am cured. I continue to hope that. I continue to realize that I should only think about it when necessary, but it is my constant subtext.

Stacy's fate was largely (not entirely) sealed when the surgery was done without the doctors knowing that the tumors were malignant. My fate was largely predictable when the doctor gave me testosterone without first doing a biopsy. And yet the majority fare better under statistical treatment models. Or the costs stay low under statistical treatment models. Or it's easier to justify statistical treatment models reducing the insurer/provider risk. I revisit all my thoughts again, hoping the conclusions will be different each iteration.

I know what to do and am seeking the controls. I don't want Deborah to read it because it seems depressing. She says it's just literature. What me worry?

This is about Stacy, about me, about us, about you. I'm suggesting that I can only know what Stacy went through by examining me and assuming we are human similar. Kim thinks I risk exposing myself this way. I recognize that we're also different. Stacy was more level, seeming on top of her game, uncommon yet reassuring about the possibilities. Her disease was uncommon. Stacy was most uncommon.

"bless"

comes from "bleeding"

subtlety's violence

Beautiful Poems for My Friends

For William Burroughs:
You were beautiful, and misunderstood
Childlike with your weapons and blond boys
And tuna fish sandwiches when we ate lunch
Shooting blow gun darts at the rats

For Leslie Scalapino:
You were beautiful, standing up
In the face of any idée fixe or bullies
Even the politics of resistance
Was worth resisting to retain diversity

For John Donne:
You were beautiful and complex
I'm never done with your sermons
And your surprise at the language you found
And where it went and hath a pleasant voyce

For Emily Dickinson:
You were beautiful, metaphysical and
Contradictory since consistency wasn't
How your mind worked, knowing others were
Different from you and night's beautiful possibility.